LET'S
ALL
DIE
HAPPY

PITT
POETRY
SERIES

ED OCHESTER
EDITOR

LET'S
ALL
DIE
HAPPY

ERIN ADAIR-HODGES

UNIVERSITY OF PITTSBURGH PRESS

Published by the University of Pittsburgh Press, Pittsburgh, Pa., 15260

10 9 8 7 6 5 4 3 2

ISBN 13: 978-0-8229-6514-5

ISBN 10: 0-8229-6514-3

Cover art: Ivan Bilibin, *Vasilisa*, 1899.

Cover design by Alex Wolfe

for my parents

I am sorry, I am concerned with that section of space which you are filling. Couldn't you move a little to one side for a minute?

▦ **Bruno Schulz,** *The Street of Crocodiles* ▦

CONTENTS

⁙ ‖ ⁙

⁙ ⦀ ⁙

LET'S
ALL
DIE
HAPPY

Of Yalta

Sure, it's all *Chekhov this* and *Chekhov that*
and I am far from the only one
to keep myself up at night
thinking about his gun,

but the man was a dreamboat,
gray eyes and smirking beard
and lips, those lips. The kind of man who,
were he now alive at the age he died,

would walk into the party, see me,
slide his eyes over the temperate steppe of my body,
then talk to my pretty friend.
Better for us both then that he's dead.

I've been rejected in two centuries, lonely
in millennia, pride of my generation.
This old story. Women who like men
love them until the men are holes

and the women turn back to bone.
Every time a man left me, I burned
something I loved until I was left
with only the gear knob of a Dodge Omni

and wine stains round my mouth.
Maybe that is not all true, or quite true,
or true in the way that you want—all I know
is we do not have to have a thing

to lose it. I mourn the children
I am too sad to have, the disappointment
of the lover I am too tired to take.
All day I feel them, their ghost limbs' need

and heat, echo of their bodies against
my teeth, their absences expanding inside me
like the flower behind a bullet,
the blood inside a lung.

Afterbirth Abecedarian

After I shoved him into the scrubbed world
before the split his leaving rent was laced,
cicatrix blooming a beaded frown, they lay the body

dead center on mine, writhing its red
evidence on my breasts, unleashing its
fury of molecules. The face

gripping onto its first feeling, a protest,
horrible misunderstanding.
I held him, spent, and knew then there are no truths,

just lungs that labor to form a breath, each one
knocking into the next, until
long trains of them

move a body along, which seems to
need explaining.
Oh, sweetness—I've looked for you so long. Body of my body, my

play at mattering. I swelled at his sight, his
querulous pout, the slick
reason. He

shunned my hopeful pink
tits, as he would keep doing,
unleashing the elegy he'd brought from such

vacancy inside me.
What did we hope to make alive here, among these
xerophytes, this crumbling? At night he cries,

yearns for the wordless to fill him, but I have
zeroes for eyes, a drawing of a heart for a heart.

In the Black Forest

Even the birds, stained black by the thumb
of morning. If not love, then at least a thing

that is not love's undoing, that is not
a lung with nothing to do. When I dream

of loving another man it is only
a muscle remembering the joy

of work. Recall our middle
fingers' calluses, toughed up

from the gripping of pens. I thought mine
would keep crusting, that I'd die with a claw

like a fruit-heavy crone, open in mid-temptation—
instead there is only bone and over it

nothing to note. Not all sentences end
in a way that sounds like knowing anything.

I have this son who tumbled out
of a Boy Scouts manual, a Little Rascal

inked to pink starring in an opera
of dirt—but he's afraid

of mean faces, stepmothers and queens
green with memories of milk skin murmurs

through lace at the nape.
It's okay, I say, they'll end up alone

dancing to death in red-hot shoes.
One day it is your finger on the spindle,

the next you are cursing the bobbin,
giving it two jobs to do. Some weeks

no one says my first name, no one's
tongue flicks the last letter out.

Tell me what sounds I look like,
what your lips do upon remembering

me, how I was last century, when I was only
practicing, when I changed the locks

because I thought there were more keys to come.

Portrait of the Mother: 1985

First there was the word and the word was *okay*.
   Okay the apartment's rented floor, new child
      laid over eyelashes and skin's salt on shag.

Okay the sleeplessness, okay the mash-mouthed hunger
   and greed, crust of milk and blood,
      pink lips pealing cooed chimes. Okay, okay

old house on dirt acre okay. Next child fat and broken,
   okay the strong arms to pull his chunk behind. Okay Disneyland
      every decade, okay man his job his money his dinner on-time

England a ghost ship on a map accent fading okay,
   R's emerging, okay the desert's branding
      the palimpsest of skin. The okay coupon shoebox,

chicken dragged through saltines/hamburger meat in milk,
   cable in the bedroom, community college class at night that once
      where is the dinner okay, him at church a deacon of backslaps,

surprise child who does not rest but foghorns through the night as if always
   on the edge of the shore's jagged crotch though this place is waterless,
      aspirational book list on the fridge, Ephesians 5:22,

broom handle's yellow paint flaking leaving a scattered golden trail,
Piggly Wiggly cart's broken wheel unlatching its throat to warble out
its weary song of lamentation, I Can't Get No Satisfaction

Muzaked from above over cans of meat and soup with noodles spun
into letters you will offer your children with both hands saying
take it, okay, this is all there is, is all that is left.

The Last Judgment

I come to you in all seriousness, reverent
as a turtleneck—I am graceless but I am not depraved.
I went to synagogues for a year because I had lost God

and was trying to find Him, following clues
with my oversized magnifying glass held up
to my giant eye, lashes collapsing like jaws, grilling congregants

under the naked lightbulb of my longing. I kept just
missing him. He went thataway. Maybe I wanted to be Jewish
to be done with Jesus but not yet break up

with God, as if moving into the guest room but leaving
my clothes in the other closet, that version of myself
a hallway away. I am the ghost of the house I live in—

old me-phantoms surround, fuck around with the furniture,
make all the mirrors tell the truth. One night I have a dream
my husband leaves and the nightmare part is that I'm

relieved and so I finally see who I am. It's not
that I got used to loneliness, only that it was too late
to learn anything else. The first time a man touched me

it was to lower me into the water and raise me out,
new fish, the sin picked clean. I was saved, as if I could be
spent—saved, I saved myself for God, or if not God

then a man God sent, posing us toward each other
in a desert diorama, His Holy Homework,
but the first two boys I loved are dead, so at night

I give myself to them, unzip the hollows, usher them into
the pitch. The books inside me are blank. I birth the boys
as my son, whom I love and yearn to forgive.

Rough Math

I woke from this dream forgetting to be not mad
but disappointed. The day shows up in corduroy again.
My mother's lost her apartment and so must move in
with her mother, who's lost everything else,
so of course I burn the calendars, every box an anniversary
of someone's greatest grief. Has someone said this
before? Can I say a new true thing, and if not—
then? What? Imagine this poem is my hand
opening. Imagine this the grenade in your chest:
pin in my teeth. I want you to hurt
and I want to know about it, want your grief
to pour from your eyes like smoke so that I may be
cool and tender. I've dreamt of you
sitting there, your various hair, that way you tilt your head
when deciding if something is bullshit. So?
The tin can is to my ear. All I hear is string.

Pantoum: For My Mother

What awaits us, after the unpetaling of her head—
a dark mound, fist in the brain,
useless save for the dark things it has made her do:
the shocks of sobbing, the razor blade

a dark mound, fist in the brain
hunked like a cruel fruit, exotic
(the shocks of sobbing, the razor blade)
pustules possible and exploding like hunger

hunked like a cruel fruit, exotic,
there for thirty years, since my conception or my birth,
pustules possible and exploding like hunger
and I cannot shake the guilt of this

there for thirty years, since my birth, my conception.
She may not remember anything of our before afterwards
and I cannot shake the guilt of this
so I must make sure to do wonderful things.

She may not remember anything of our before afterwards
if she comes out at all, skinned open and sewn back
so I must make sure to do wonderful things,
her life bursting and scorching the stuff of this place.

If she comes out at all, skinned open and sewn back,
I promise to help her cut up and eat this town,
her life bursting and scorching the stuff of this place—
none of this did what it should, stupid and cruel.

I promise to help her cut up and eat this town,
steal maybe, maybe burn down or screw.
None of this did what it should, stupid and cruel
and I want to be stupid and cruel, too—
.

steal maybe, maybe burn down or screw
something with some fight in it, because
I want to be stupid and cruel, too,
and not this heavy, not an afraid thing

but something with some fight in it, because it's
useless to save the dark things it has made her do.
Not so heavy. Nothing. Not afraid
of what awaits us after the unpetaling of her head.

Everybody in the Car
We Are Leaving without You

Let's all die happy.
Let's all take our lactose intolerance pills
& move to Milwaukee, home school our kids
with curds. Let's be white & rich & give away
all our homes in which we have replaced the furniture
with replicas of ¾ size. Let's unlearn mayonnaise.
Let's apply for the job, fly to the place of the job,
interview for the job, get the job, then tell them
to go fuck themselves, we don't need a job.
Let's reanimate Robert Frost.
Let's switch New Mexico & Arizona to see
if anyone notices. Let's pine panel our Volvos.
Let's vacuum the stars, charting their whir
around the dust canister of eternity. Let's be
a sweet shop in Vienna. Let's be Vienna. Let's learn
the whole room's names & mix them up on purpose.
Let's be purpose. Let's be accident, not all, just those
that maim. Let's speak the language
of clocks & grass & graves. Let's set Whitman
& Dickinson up on a date & watch
as the awkwardness flames. Let's be hungry & not eat,
be revolutions without names. Let's all be the lake
that the bodies go into, opening its jaws
without love, without blame.

On a Line Overheard in a Crowd of Middle School Cheerleaders

I love you, but your nails are a nightmare

and there is something savage inside each of us
that makes us bend into glyphs and yell the names
of the animals who would take our skin not to love
but to wear into the night. If there are five chairs
we will fit onto them ten, our skinny legs bending
into laps for the small and golden. There is nothing
on this earth we cannot change. Where once dragons
smelt arcs of rocks into sand there now stands
a smoothie shop pedaling sweetness only because
we are hungry. Our bodies keep the night awake
with worry. Under your tongue is the hollowed place
we crawl into and whisper out embarrassing things
that sting like a citrusy truth. Whose idea do you think
it was to raise the roof, to let it burn? Who else
could have invented California? These are terrible times
to be alive if you are anyone else,
the world an unthimbled thumb and we the glorious pins.

The Jennifer Century

America! Give to me your 200 years
of names borrowed from the Bible. Anyone
can be a Mary. Australians. A Canadian.
Take instead the all-American sound
of *Jennifer*. Feel how it Kansases
in your mouth, a flat rectangle of democracy.
Notice in it the guttural yearn,
primal urge for curds, conspicuous consumption
of the doubled-n. Leave for the limeys
their *Guinevere*, to the Cornish *Gwenhwyfar*,
the origin stories too. America
did not rise, enfogged, from a lake,
was not pulled from a stone by a king.
We emerged from the stocked shelves
of Spencer's Gifts and More,
from the aisle of black lights and St. Patrick's Day
shirts festooned with "I'm So Irish, My Liver Hurts"
and "Erin Go Braless." Give to our Jennifers
the American J, so goddamned unique
the Commies have nothing like it
and which the French mispronounce.

O beautiful Jennifers, for spacious Camaros,
for amber waves of perms. May you crack
your gum forever, the canyons and forests
and food courts echoing with its snap,
Haileys and Kaylees circling the edges,
watching for the moment your fringed jackets drop
to paw the ground and pounce.

I Would Have Listened to Rush

I would have slit the throat of morning,
would have loaded the lifeboats with lions.
I would have burned the books
I'd found myself in, making for you
bouquets from the flames. For you,
I would have been thin, eventually,
for you would have been my bread.
I would have charted the phases
of your lazy eye, waxing crescent
of love, waning gibbous of desire.
I would have left paradise, or at least
Prague. I would have stayed with you
in the desert, wandering, tending
your father's pecan trees,
balming the stump of your abuelo's
severed arm. I'd have eaten
the menudo we made,
the offal on my lips
a way of loving you.
I would have made myself be strong
so that when you ruined me,
it meant something.

Once I Was a Thimble but Now I Am a Bell

What are the words for I how I feel today?
Beer can in the drainage ditch,
a litter of smittens, sunburned slash
where no arms could reach.
The morning wears last night's mascara
and I can be anything I want—
happy. Guilty. A certain kind of free,
as if the day is a car to which I have
keys. As if there is a road.
But I am February's bone,
its marbled mate, de-leafed and
trembling. I was made in the image
of an image, grown hazy in translation
and a little bit of a lie. The good news
is that someday I may learn my lesson, but
the blood I make isn't a reminder
nor is it the sin. It is the clanging—
not the hunger
but the promise of hunger to come.

Domestic Geography

My father has only work/church dress Wranglers so when he relaxes at home he wears
just underwear

shirt and shorts, white and white on white. I am in training and must fold them.
The only time we are close.

We think the neighbor boy shows my baby sister his penis, but we are not sure.
He becomes a man and dies in Iraq

like lots of people. My father served in Asia but did not fight in any way
they give medals for.

At home everything is about *jotos*: Batman and Joto, Michael Jackson Joto,
Luke Jotowalker.

I cry though I am not sure why. I cry for Ethiopia and save my change in a Folgers can. I cry
for Charlie Brown

not the football part, which it seems like he deserves, but for when he gets
no valentines.

I have a brother who goes away and a father who lets him. I use the Africa money
to wish him back,

standing at the lip of the mall's lazy fountain to pour in coins. They sink to the bottom,
faces of the dead just staring.

Nuestra Señora de Belén

Pito-Pito roams the streets on invisible missions, sack over shoulder that slaps on his back, filled with whispers of baby doll heads/ roadkilled cats. Tin cans, says my dad. Tanya says in there is a junkyard of ghosts, that when your fractions or friendship pins or Star Wars thermos go missing they are not real gone, only taken by Pito-Pito for fuel. She is so mean everything sounds true. Junior high girls say they saw his *verga*, crooked and slick, beckoning. Pito-Pito, I am a tooth like you. The train at night so loud I am inside the sound. I have secrets, Pito-Pito. I practice disappearing. I was born in a bindle on the knuckle of the world.

Girl, know your history.

Belén, New Mexico

You are here because of men, mostly
    white men who wagoned and clopped,

    jumped from boxcars into the dirt
toting seed from which you sprung

in the young state, old place, four nations now
    at least. Just because you were named

    for the island you look like don't mean
you belong there. Open your eyes, blue

and black. You didn't even take
    Spanish, so sure you were

    you'd leave. *Que estupida.*
All your fathers left, killed, came back,

ate their medals and punched
    the mouths they loved.

    Go to the ocean. There is not water
enough to remake you.

You didn't move out of this town.
    This town moved into you.

Consumption

During the war, this grandfather goes west
to the east, and when he returns, the man finds his wife
has frocked their son in lightness and lace.
The boy calls his mom's father *Daddy*.

The things the man had had to do.
That you could unpeel a person from his body.

Years later, the new children come out so fair
the boy is now the dark one, *Injun*
an aunt will say with a sniff, though she is too
and knows it. He gets pushed out of a window,

out of time. He runs to the Navy
and its easy love. Each day's chores are chances

and he is free, free in the salt and ocean,
swimming out to meet the sun like a man
and the water loves him back, wants to marry him,
have him take its name, but he doesn't know how

to be so adored. The ocean spits him out,
crying into the shore, taking his breath as it leaves.

That's where they find him.
Sand-crusted mothers flutter, practicing
the anecdote of the dead man, seaweed crowned,
when a dentist who has longed

to be brave
pushes his mouth

onto my father's mouth
pounding out water from his lungs,
breathing into them fresh air
and tuberculosis,

hands engining the heart,
saving my father to death.

Wedding Polaroid '75

Who remembers the real sky?
This day seen here is a haze,
sun grinning through a mouthful of dirt

a party in the park
at the end of the world.
The film split, cracked, yellow veins

colonizing the dark where trees
must have been, menacing
the face of the woman

in a straw hat with ribbons
and the man to her right,
dark for all the white he's wearing.

There is no music anywhere
and the couple's clothes are chemicals
the creeping night can't breathe through

but there is somewhere a bottle of champagne
that will appear in other photos
to bring its cold joy. He will take the first

sip and offer her the next which is how
it will always be but she lets the bubbles
whisper otherwise until it feels like

happiness and the wine slides down
into the space she keeps empty,
then to where I, red storm, am growing.

Afterlife

Which wife will wait for you
there, beyond all of this solidness?

Which woman will you ask
to carry your glasses

in her purse, forgetting
to leave your body's breaking

behind? Who would take you
on, again, knowing?

Or maybe it will be you
making meals to order,

starching collars in the spectral flicker
of eternity's situation comedies.

To the moon, the box bellows,
the iron shaking in your hand.

The Robin Tanka

Shit on a shingle
Salisbury steak, chicken fried
steak, meat pounded thin
dredged through egg and saltines, the
meat is cheap she does not eat

⣿

When she comes to my
office so I can help her
file paperwork for
disability I don't
introduce her to my friends

⣿

She's written down the
password wrong, can't write in script
anymore so now
everything scrawled from her hand
looks like warnings, lettered teeth

⠿

There were two turns. She
was confused and took the first
though what I wrote was
second. She shrugs. *I*
thought I knew the way to go

⠿

I remember what
it was like to love her
easily, to feel
intended, born of her dead
tooth, green eyes I'd kiss to dry

⠿

She never goes back
to where she's born. The desert
thorns up around her.
Her voice is a music box
grown tired of being turned

···

In the morning they
will slice her skin and tear out
her womb, boot where I
grew into her ruin. She's
marked me down as next of kin

···

I turn her into
the bird of her name, hold her
red in my hand. I
open my mouth to feed her
music, dark notes tumbling

···

In pre-op, tented
and clean. They bring in some clouds
and she waves to me.
I am the forest she made,
wolf. I am her breadcrumbs, too

The High School Principal's Daughter

At high school games I flash my name
and suck up licorice for free—concession
girls teasing bangs, readying their eyeliner
and asses for the gang press of halftime,
sticky carnival of flesh. Beer-blooded stomps
see me and run as if my eyes
have teeth to tattle but some stare, the orange
caution cones around me a dare,
and they crush their pelvises into my
waist, asking to whom I belong. Of course
they don't say *whom*—they slur *You're his*
daughter. You're his kid, you're getting
big and offer me a drink. I like biting
the ends off licorice ropes and using
them for straws, slurping soda, the sugar
mumbling my bones. In the night halls
I spin the locker codes as if I belong
inside, push past typewriters covered
like widows and into my father's
office to sit behind his desk,
the wooden paddle in my hands
heavy and worked to a shine.

The Trap

There is no greater tragedy than to be young
and think you know what joy will look like, and so clunk and pigeon
through corridors and malls, flapping against the linoleum
of heartbreak—the map you found, dirty with the fingerprints
of just everyone, held to your chest like a rosary or a stake—
peeking into chemistry classrooms and corn dog stands,
hot on joy's musky scent. You could have sworn
you just saw it, over here, by the fire extinguisher
on whose painted door someone has carved *I fucked Jenny*
in letters hinged like blades, lightning bolts angry and bored.
You think you know joy's habitat, its sleeping patterns,
on what it needs to feed, and so imagine setting up the lure, trap
jaws snapping on joy's fat middle and it's yours, its body
and sickness too. Maybe you try to bait yourself, supine
you glisten with newness, the borrowed body you wear
vibrating its need. It's so loud you think it could rechart rivers.
You worry for flora and their thirst, wonder how anyone sleeps
with the sound of you crashing in their happy ears.

[1987]

Girls wore their jeans
rolled tight at the bottoms

as if staunching an angry wound
and I did not know how to do this.

Nights I practiced the tender operation,
the seam staying shut for a charmed moment

in which I could see all the possible versions
of myself go forward, alive and not

ashamed of that. The god I loved was the god
of everything—God of Line Length at Tastee-Freeze,

Lord of the On-time School Bus, Almighty
King of Hair Feathering, Glorious Light That Shines

onto Us and Reveals a Boy's Love For Me
Someday Please—bearded voice

loosing stentorian rumbles in the summer sky,
glasses low on a star-dusted nose, nothing

was too small for his care. Loved, I stood
up from peach carpet to take my place,

the cuffs sighing with exhaustion
and the unraveling began.

Judy Chicago

moves into the Belen Hotel
where during The War whores
greet GIs to tenderly/roughly
fuck/blow depending on the depth
of the deposit. The train pukes
them out by the score where men
like my great-uncle wait
to lead them down the street
and into their forgetting.
By the end, they are all old
or else so young the women coo
at such smoothness, rubbing
their hands over farms of chests,
soft acres of innocence.
Or the new soldiers are not this at all.
They're juvenile delinquents,
slicked hair buzzed to a shadow
they'll carry with them
into the bombed ribs of churches,
hollowing flesh, turning the world
to ghosts. Or maybe
the great-uncle I mentioned is not yet
the muscle for the town's bookies
and pimps. Maybe he is still in Guadalcanal

where the only thing worse
than what he does
is what he sees done.
He wears the brains of friends for days.
When he returns, he finds in beating
the faces of men
with sticks and fists and baseball bats
a music. He lets their bones rise a bit
so as to slap them down,
the thwap of flesh on the floor
deepening as the song goes.
The hardwood darkens—
flowers form and thorn.
When Judy Chicago
buys the hotel it has been abandoned
my whole life, broken windows
winking at the street,
bird shit veining the halls.

Twelve

I pull from the nut an ashing tree
to shade the baking hill
and follow the ants as they drill
for attacks by the hungry or curious
or cruel the summer Tara Calico
is killed we think or just taken

we pray. Dad puts on his boots
to walk his way into the desert
that swallows her bike and body.
The town's men make a chain.
It turns fall and her trail's rained away.

I am twelve and in my head
is a dirigible beginning its soft exploding.
Whatever is happening to me
no one can see. I eat the windows
and brick up the doors.

::::

Jesus is listening. He can't help it—
that's part of the deal. But maybe Jesus
is hiding like me in a closet

for some privacy from the clamor
of his eternal family, his own Walkman
turned on and up and blaring the songs
he's found to soundtrack the playact
of his days. If he's feeling tricky
maybe it's "Stairway," and he makes appear
in his wounded hands
a Schecter Diamond Series Blackjack
Stratacaster-style guitar to shred the solo
to death, his blood on the strings.

⁝⁝

(I am forming in the night.
Trains unloose their throats
and I crawl in. We are announcing
our love. The silence after
is bigger, a lung expanding
to the size of the room.
My sister rolls into me—
I bleed all over her,
bird made of thorns.)

⁝⁝

Is it winter yet when the boy pushes me
against the neighbor's garage,
prying open my small mouth
with his tongue, fat and I swear even
sweaty? Have the birds yet left
behind only a silence
that through absence
makes its presence felt?
And what kinds of birds are those
anyway—I don't know the names
of anything. Am I still
wearing the dusty rose coat,
or is this the time he throws it
in the dirt? Am I still frozen
under the meat of his want
or is my father's voice booming
my three names into the desert?
Have I not yet started running
into the angry dusk of God?

⁙

I have moved into *Jane Eyre*
to try a different sort of darkness

and seek sick friends to save.
Dear Diary, I have named our house

Goatheadfield. I am certain this is
hilarious but my friend who reads

has moved away and my mother
has some things to do

so there's no way to know for sure.
I taste the gruel, practice

the moors. I hate the greed
of Bertha's insanity because I think

I know what kind of adult
I will grow up to be.

⁙

We make bouquets
from what we find,

pull the loveliest plants
around. We do not understand

their names are *scorpionweed,*
hog potato, devil's beggarticks.

We do not know yet
to despise them,

such loose and easy blooming.

⁘

My cousins raise the pig
and their tio slices
its throat, blood caught
in an old Tupperware saved
for this day. When we arrive
the pig is spinning. The long swine
shines to a crisp. They release
the chicharrones first,
bright stars of fat. The men smell
of flesh and steel. The women
hum in the kitchen and I go in not to help
but to watch my mother,
British and pale, fail at sopaipillas.

:::

In P.E. they take us to Sugar Lanes
fifty feet from the Belen Hotel
which sits like a rumor
on an old tongue,
aching to be told.
Girls fight over the six-pound ball
so I pull out the eight.
Though I am not strong
I want to be. I'm getting worn down
by the weakness I see.

:::

Betty Friedan I have found you
stained and dusty, fallen
behind my home's small bookcase.
You've been pressed into a pair of wings.

Betty Friedan I was wondering
if you could come and get me.
I don't have much to pack
and I am afraid if, I am afraid

every day that I will wake up
and still be here. You know what it is,
don't you, to be stuck inside
your life, though you don't remember

walking in? Ma'am, I am trying
to be good, good enough
to see in space, good enough for God
to tear a hole in this town

for me to crawl out of. I keep writing
down what I hear. They found it
and the seams on our house
exploded. Betty Friedan they've hidden

the door so I have moved into a lung.
The blackness wants me
to learn its name and I am trying
but there are no notes to pass my lips

only a symphony of bones.

I Am Twenty-One

and my roommate is a man
so beautiful he is not expected
to say anything true. We sleep

separated by the suggestion
of a door. He is so close
I hear his hard-ons and he my

scabbing. I walk through his room
to get to the loo during the deep pocket
of night through which he cocoons

in a plaid of streetlights
strained through bars. I think everything
is practice and so I let myself love him

a little, both what is there and what I just
make up, and I get so good at it I forget
I am loving a ghost. Sing to me, ghost,

I say. We've forgotten to pay
for everything—our lives candles
on cardboard boxes, hot wax bleeding

through the slits. There's lipstick
on the wine bottle, jizz and toast
in the sink. Nights I hear him pounding

blondes through the hung-up sheet
I leave for the streets and look for a bruise
to walk into. I come back when the cats

have begun their morning hate
under the house and up in the walls,
bodies full of fever and singing.

Lookback

I thought I loved God and His son
and all of that stuff
but I may have just liked being good

at Church, A-pluses in verses, hymns,
virginity-maintaining, I was always The Mary,
The Angel wearing white bedsheets and gold

bric-a-brac, bringing God's lava voice
to hunkering stables of men. I loved Him
like a savings account, feeling holy

in my asceticism but waiting for the day
I could go to the Bank of Eternal Good Things
(main branch), cross its marble floors,

slide the withdrawal slip to the teller and cart off my bags
of dry humping and smooth skin.
Tolstoy believed something else

about the loving of this God, but by the time
I knew who Tolstoy was I didn't care
what he had to say about gods, only people,

the reasons they wake up in the morning
to seas of golden wheat
then burn the country down. But God

cannot be separated from Tolstoy
just because He was separated from me.
Did Lev love God because he walked around

in His holy likeness, white man with white beard:
wise, unpredictable, and given
to the wearing of linen? Would I still love Him

if He were Her— cranky and jealous,
redheaded and bored? But isn't that God?
My whole dumb life I have loved people into leaving,

flooding my heart's high school with a fire
I stand inside, alone and made of salt.

Neighborhood Watch

It is spring and the drug dealer's shorts are white,
as are the sunglasses he wears on the back
of his neck, as if to say he sees the dogs who hunt

to harm him. I call the police every few months,
solstice and equinox. It is Albuquerque,
now famous to America

for a t.v. show about a dying teacher
compelled to make meth, driven by the lack
of a single-payer health care system

and his own heretofore suppressed megalomania.
The car wash which serves as metaphor
is behind my brother's house, the kingpin's chicken shack

our breakfast burrito place. His apprentice is said to live
in a house next door to my best friend's grandmother
and the hero kills this assistant's girlfriend in an apartment

I went to a party at once. Visitors pay to ride
in a wan RV like the one the white actors
cook drugs in. It stops to let tourists out to pose,

reenact famous scenes. Across from our house
on Christmas Eve, we see the drug dealer
pound his fists into his girlfriend's head. My son

is coloring in reindeer, some elves. When the police arrive
the woman is gone then nothing happens.
We watch the show and I cannot tell from where
all the gunshots are coming.

American Idyll

My son says he's Iron Man and I'm not sure
he's not, so I listen to him. But he's three
and would point us always west, driving
over salt flats and into the ocean's hunger.
I've been put here to protect him from his desires.
For years I knew the world from the backseat
of an eye-shadow blue Oldsmobile, mutinous shopping carts
never seen from a distance but only as we passed
and turned them to dirt behind us.
Some days, I'd open the door of the garage
to breathe in the smell of gas—patchwork fur coat
in my lungs—climb into the car, play the chromed
radio buttons, and sing into the gear shift
songs of racial harmony and roller skating
before gripping the finger-grooved wheel,
pointing it at places like a possibility machine.
In the sitcom theme song of my life
there would be driving,
quick cuts of my glossed face
and sunset hair feathering along the clouds
as my convertible lapped monorails and cruised 66
to the black eye of the moon.
Future music blaring from the speakers,
a man doing something to my right.
The world gets out of the way of what I want.

Natural History

Mostly he is a meteor—churning past displays
on how this desert was once the floor
of an ocean, wet once if only for an eon—
before he pauses near a replica of the front foot
of a Brachiosaurus, thinking, maybe, of our smallness,

but probably not. Smallness is to him temporary,
a stage to transcend before entering the world of men
like a fist. Every day I watch his preparation,
the caped spectacle, and worry not for him
but for those he is born to bruise. In a liquid room,

lights impersonate waves
he sinks down in to swim, sons
of our friends following in his wake,
arms bent and threshing the ground,
a school of disaster engines. He leads us

to a room of flames, end of the world
flickering on just one wall.
Asteroids rain and punch the earth.
Is that what happened he asks *to turn the dinosaurs
into bones?* We say *Yes*, though what takes us

doesn't matter. No one's death is a lesson
for the living. There is nothing else we know
for sure. His fingers turn claws as the film
starts again and we wait for his favorite part,
the hungry meat, in the sky a coming fire.

Ode to My Dishwasher

It is late, my love, and you are loud,
worrying at your work. I know
I should ask you to leave, to join
your vintage in a salvage yard,
hitch with kin on a truck to Juárez.
My mother says I deserve better

but I do not think I do.
For twenty years I lived without you
or the steam our love would bring
and in this way I was a little more
in the world or at least
I thought this sometimes

as I offered to the sink
a furious bounty of glass.
To be a grown woman, alone
and unclean is a powerful thing.
My mother had so many rubber gloves.
I was surprised by the sight of her hands

which seemed to me old
even when she was young
and so I thought I did not want to get old
but now I know I did not want to get old
while doing the dishes. I did not think
I would marry but when I did

it was to a man who finds in the soaping
and scrubbing a kind of quiet glory.
He stands with his hands in the water
to clean what cannot be loaded,
what he has saved from your center,
cleft into which I have stuffed everything.

Consume

At our wedding I wore blue.
We danced so much we forgot

about the cake and that cutting it
should have some meaning, as if to say

we will go through the world together,
holding on to a tool made for one,

thereby making simple tasks
inordinately difficult and cumbersome,

this shared frustration
at the chore of modern life

binding us, giving to us
dinner conversation for years,

united in hating the same things.
So we said *fuck it* and ate the cake

with our hands, our family of friends
and blood winding their way back

to the night jaws which had loosed them.
Chocolate in our bed.

In the morning I woke to you,
smear of jam on your face—

wolf that has devoured
the fattest doe in the field.

The New Year

We don't realize it's midnight until the gunfire,
erupting like acne across the unscrubbed streets,

waves of it rising to meet each other, two oceans jealous
of each other's thunder. I'm trying to say something

about hopelessness, how it's not always an absence but rather
an opening. I know how little the accident of my existence

deserves. My son was born on my birthday—a lesson
dipped in blessing. I am made of only so much

paper: to draw him I had to erase some of my lines.
Up close the smudges look like shadows though

it's hard to say from where the light to make them shines.
When I jog it is not for health or happiness but

to prepare for the apocalypse, to outrun whatever comes—
the first lesson I learned was that no one takes you in,

no matter how heavy with miracle you are, leaving you to lie
in a barn, blood in the straw, birthing your own salvation.

Vow

This city's twenty miles across from tit to toe,
something I'm told
my grandfather would have said,

the one I didn't know and could not
have loved, so who needs him here?
When he died in '69 his wife went too,

throwing her heart into the protestant hole,
her body following thirty years later.
I do not love you like this.

Sometimes, while driving past strip malls
chained like verses of campground rounds,
I think of your death, not the fall

or a crash but the call when they find
Wife in your phone and I imagine
I'll know from the tone of the stranger's voice

asking if I belong to your name. I'll know
the fact but not the feelings, which I'm bad at
and so have to rehearse but I think first

of money, how there is none. I'd have to leave
the house in a month and mourn you
in an apartment, maybe in a complex

with a pool. Mornings after I cross alive
over the guilty river of night, our son
might ask to swim, his grief a thing

just budding its teeth, and I will take him
down to the water, float his body like a lamp
I am offering to the other side.

My Son, the Night Light, the Dark

La tortuga carries all the stars on her back—
they burst from humps of shell and shine
the blue room with stories, the bear

on his eternal hunt, Cassiopeia drowsy
and expectant with tragedy. Buttons
change the hue—green, gold, the purple

of a bruise. He asks me to lie with him
until the stars disappear. I have things
to do, corners of myself to crawl into,

but I lay my body next to his and ask him
what he sees in his head. No one, he whispers,
likes me. As if he's read from the book

I wrote. I press him into me to swallow
such words and remind him he was invented
to be loved. He is five and wishes he wasn't

alive. The black claw
scuttles from its clamp inside me, peeks
from my throat to creep through his lips,

moving from the husked host to suck
his marrow, so glittering it pounds
through his skin. I can save my love

from nothing, not the bad blood
that's beat my heart to scab,
not the grief ribboning my milk.

Regeneration

Forgiven, my father says he struggled
to not hit us the way his father
had punched and smacked and kicked him

and so my father is a man who had thought
of putting his boot to my head. When my son
pushes me saying   *not you   not mama   go away*

I think of giving in to him, leaving
in the old way/cheap gas way, driving until all
is borderless and taking with me

only impractical clothes. After he was born
I did not want to die but nor
did I exactly want to not-die so I imagined

escaping to Prague, getting skinny,
and wearing knee-high boots
as I walked the languorous walk

of those who have somewhere to go
and all the time to arrive, over the city's
storied skin bulging with violins

and sadness, kavarnas exhaling smoke,
drunks spitting come-ons because it is late
and I am beautiful and I am alone.

In a Dry County

The restaurant sells beer but you have to be in a club

    how do I get in the club I ask
                you have to tell me you want to be in
                the club, she says
OK, I say, yes
                you have to say it, she says

it is like we are getting married or I am giving her
a Miranda warning
    I want to be in the club, OK, now what, how much
                it's free you're in the club
    OK but how do I get out
                you can't get out it's for always, you are
                always in this club
    but what if I never come back, my father is very old
    and he's why I'm here and I am trying to bring him back
    to New Mexico to live as long as he can live.

She is so young she thinks people only die in car accidents.

                It's OK, she whispers, you're still in the club.

Near Forty

It is not the year of cancer, which was last year—
harmonizing ovarian odes, lymphomic hymns,
the discordant kicked out and mourned—but it is the year
of splintering, of love's sparrow bones giving way.
It is the season of early autism intervention, of rehab, of owning
a funeral dress. The day of child custody agreements
has dawned, pink light of co-parenting cresting.
It is not yet the year of remarriage, of blending,
of unlatching and rehyphening, nor yet the time
of filling the spare room with mementos meant
to trigger a memory for the parent returning
from a sunlit inland to the foggy creep of shore.
It is, however, the year of final children or the planned
and yearned for first, also the goodbye to all that stuff.
It is the year of now or never, the see-saw of somedays
and back-whens flattening. Now is the hour of committing
seriously to pastimes and paths that lead away from
the thorny forest of the soul into an even and unearthly
light. This is the age of replacements, the future's loosening,
and of the body's ripening song.

The Mammogram

Welcome to the club the technician says,
my left breast in her hand.

But you're a little young, she adds, and it's true
yet in the a.m.'s probe and pat

there had been a lump, a knob,
a star nova-ing into nothing.

I had been a girl for so long.
In gym I craved the secret hair

and whispered need
of a welcome gift for Aunt Flo,

cigar for Uncle Red,
clucked jive of our tribe.

I even once asked
a semi-popular girl to pass

me a pad, to smuggle
it to me in math. *For what?*

she laughed,
Arts and crafts?

I had been made, caught
as a fraud and so when

the blood and pain finally came
I thought it meant moving

into my life, an ivy-crossed, bricked-loft,
eastern city life—an argyle man

important books in hand,
hands on my slender body life—

a loud life, a rain life,
a lived in this world life—

as if that's what blood could bring.
I have never even been to New York City.

It kept changing without me there
and now the place I was meant to be is gone

and so I don't live anywhere.
I've been thinking a lot about desire

and how—driving this station wagon
into the middle of my life—

I miss it not just in me
but in the men around me, men

my age who pass me by
because I remind them of their wives,

who think they know
what my breasts would feel like

in their mouths hot with sighs,
dropping a little from the bridge of bra

into the normal night,
child asleep in the other room,

laundry at the foot of the bed.
I forgive you.

I forgive you, men,
for abandoning your arrows

in the fleshy apple of my heart.
I forgive you for squandering

your beauty first and demanding it still
of me. I would do the same,

so I forgive myself, too. When my son
was young, pink worm, he spurned

my breasts, he clawed my flesh.
We bound his arms so he'd still to drink

from the reddening pink, my body aching
to let go its gift. As he fed on my left,

my right would release, jealous
or maybe just lonely,

my skin covered in all kinds of tears.
I had pushed him out for hours

or years, his bones tearing through
the slips. Undrugged, I felt the needle

stitch the slice like the frowns of skin
where my father's mother's breasts

had been. Nothing was put back.
She hadn't been using them anyway,

she said, her husband dead and sons
full grown. Maybe that's who she thought

breasts were for. After the Scythians cut down
fields of foreign men, their own women turned

and wiped out their mates,
nulling the will of fortune or fate,

each carving out her own right breast
so nothing would stop the death

she'd bring, the left saved
to nurse the girls, the boys slain.

I let my own son see me change,
watch me dress, see my breasts.

Soon I must stop and close the door
of my body to him but if I am ever old

he may have to hold them
in his hands again

to clean the underneath. If I prayed,
it would be for this: not to not yet die

but to have loved him into a man
who would take the wizened wrecks

of his mother's sex with such tenderness
that the stars tear off their faces and sing.

The Confessions

I was married to a bonfire,
  raised whirligigs in Spain.
I invented Herman Melville
  as a way to say something about capitalism

but now America is a vanity license plate
  only the driver can decode. I swooned once
for a dictator who promised me portraiture

on valueless currency—now I'm heavy with coin
  and exile. Young, I was seduced
by The Unofficial Jane Austen Tarot Pack©,
  Darcy Celtic-crossing my Fanny Price,

and threw over several beige men
  for one made of lightning and croquembouche.
Speaking in French, I don't,

save on my résumé which reads
  like a list of what I've settled for.
I'd been lately seeking a position
  as a cotton nightgown but don't have

the material—can't compete with the high-
        necked tricks, their wattles of lace. My last gig
was as a band T-shirt souvenired

from a two-week fling, loved
        until I was see-through. I could not find
my matter. I thought I'd left my body
        somewhere and like a drunken weathervane

kept asking men if they could see me.
        I was not who the mirror insisted.
A flickering, waking in white alone, I wandered

riverbanks for my children, turning my talons to twigs
        their flesh kept slipping through so I wept, no—
I howled. I screamed until I turned into wind, into myth
        bloodied up and told to girls to keep them

mouse and chaste, evidencing the fire
        in my skin, that I was burned
and became the burning.

Sonnet in XY

Napping on the couch, I am a man
answering the Manifest Destiny
of my rest, my slouch and sprawl indifferent
to the day and its mouthy demands. I
am tired therefore I sleep. Is this what
it is like to see a woman's thigh, top-
dome of her breast, thinking it calls to you,
singing your name across the caring galaxy?

Manned, I charge into the night armed
with only the gun of my body—no
keys laced between fingers, no look backs/walk
fasts. No staying in the light. I walk
into the dark because it loves me.
I am the first word it ever said.

A Murder of Librarians

for Amy

having suitably sucker-punched the night
the tequila talked off the table   we are back
to the stuff of our bones   we shove fists
into each other and pour lead into the dents
they make   it's true we exist   you say
it's a good idea to break a bottle, hold it like a crucifix
if what we ward away would harm us, then that's evil alright
                you say let's make some veins sing
all over el patio, mujeres thrum   their men dance before the end
of our stares, hyenaed   we take the women
two by two   pulling them into our betweens
letting their softness bully us
                then we take the men
you're barrel-walking and proud of my pockmarks
and suddenly the guns in our hands
have somewhere they need to be   the sky is laughable
it doesn't know what dark is   the wind of me is older
than the name of here, and we own each other
i was here before the stars
you shoot in the air   the saddle between my legs works
like a miracle   we name our horses accordingly
you start to feel like all the dirt in the world

Pisces

Kurt Cobain, Patty Hearst, and I
walk into our birthday bar where it's playing
our favorite song, where it smells like lime and piss

got into a fight from which no winner
has emerged. We order bourbon
because we were born in a winter

that's never left our bones,
ice in our laughs but not in our glasses
which we take neat and mean. Kurt asks me

what it's like to have gotten so old
though he was here first. I tell him
it's like a bouquet of Mondays,

the alarm going off though we just fell
asleep. I don't want him to think
he's missing anything. Patty's smile

is a turnstile and there's a tiger stuck
in the teeth. She yells out punchlines but won't tell
the jokes and I leave to make love

to the jukebox—it's got some secrets I need—
so Kurt turns into an ellipsis, dots rolling
all over the floor. By the door, a crowd of people

peer from the street because they think   .
our sadness means we know something
true. Maybe we do. The moose head

calls from the wall, orders flutes of booze
on fire and inside us there is finally
a glowing which cannot stick

and we puke up an apocalypse,
all the music ever made
stumbling from our dead and dying mouths.

In Barstow

I was in-between emotions,
the night a tube sock
of doom! Well probably just
boredom! Also that heat!
It was the hinge of my life
maybe, how do I know
until the end what the middle was
and why not that night in Barstow
the butt crack of California
in a Super 8 alone reading a book
of *Jing Si Aphorisms* found suffocating
the Bible—*Even the tiniest bolt*
must be screwed on tightly
in order to perform its best
it said and I needed comfort but all
I got was stuck on *screwed*
which is what I wanted but also how
I felt that summer I did not move
to Portland again, the summer
of almosts, crab grass choking
the hyssop and sage with its homely
greed and who can blame crab grass
for seeing something beautiful
then stepping on its throat.

There are so many tiny murders.
It's why handjobs were invented
and I am a scientist inventing
new ways to be lonely.
I get bonuses every year.
That year, July was pressing
its mean heat to the door, listening
for a heartbeat inside and I thought
how wonderful to be wanted
through all the meat straight
to the marrow and July said *yes*
July said *whatever it is you are thinking*
I am thinking too so I tore off my clothes
to get closer, the book of aphorisms yelling
If we can reduce our desires there is nothing
really worth getting upset about but I don't like
being told what to do and out of spite
started wanting everything I saw—
popcorn ceilings! Unremovable
hangers! Stains of strangers' failures!
The room shrugged. The shag
carpet yawned and swallowed my name.

Fallen

Why not bend over for a new man
if that's what the body
beginning its back nine
is least bored by? What charity is there
in turning flesh to February
because you promised to swear off spring?
When I was young I was so good
no one dared want me like my honor
could save us all but some still died
their guns and cars colliding
blood and bone in the bottle
as if we could die from living
too much, a surplus of touch
and now I'm being pressed
against a mirror so hard I can't see
myself, just the dark center of my eye
pulling me in like I'm being unborn.

Seeing Ex-Boyfriends

Sometimes you see the young man you knew
inside the skin of this deflated one,

punk in pleats, bekhakied skater,
as if he has been drugged and eaten

by a mid-level manager not out of hunger
but rather boredom.

Sometimes, you look good, never better.
Mostly you do not.

Once, it is in traffic, you singing along
to Salt-N-Pepa, he in a car far nicer

than the rusting truck in which he took
your good bra as a trophy, hanging it

from the antenna, donuting the Kmart parking lot
the night you learned smoking was a good way

to kill time between disasters. Sometimes,
it is at a party you did not want to go to,

hair unwashed, skirt unpressed, crust of spit-up on your neck,
so that when you see him, though he is fatter and fading,

you think of why you stayed those extra months,
the gentleness with which he parted you,

and your full breasts let down their milk.

Self-Portrait as Banshee

The then-boyfriend driving my car back from Vegas
hits an elk outside of Gallup, twilight bruising the cliffs,
and we spin around just once before the ditch opens
    to take us, "Superfreak" the soundtrack to the splintering,

and a twang in white socks stops to perform his human
duties, saying he saw us clip the buck's ass but it up and ran,
    you didn't get to keep the horns or nothing. So for months

I bus to work though scores of questionably intentioned men
stop to ask if I need a ride, the daily slide up to the curb
and chivalric offering of lances. Sirs! I am the direct descendant
    of Robert the Bruce, Scottish king, liberator from English

tyranny! Lords of Annandale and Spennithorne! They
were born in Highland castles and I am sitting on gum! Oh,
    sad apple. Switchblade men size me up for a bite. Wasn't I born

on this bus, or have I not been born yet? Is this the blood tunnel into
my becoming, or out of it? For someone alive I am good at death—
not the elk but everything else, the boys I touched to dust.
    When I love you I see your bones, the stones

around your name, and I learn what I am for, not to long for
but to warn, to throat out some keening over the city,
   diaphanous and combing my long red hair.

Pilgrimage

Haven't we all moved to Poland
to be closer to seriousness

only to find it stuffed with puppets
and Bon Jovi tribute bands?

Who among us hasn't ordered
piñatas by the score, authentic

from the Mexican store, just
to leave them sitting empty

as an operating metaphor?
Every time we meet I learn new ways

to leave you, the goodbyes distinctive
and precious as hurricanes.

It is someone's job
to give these farewells names:

The Albuquerque Adios,
the Budapest Buh-Bye, Tucson Toodle-oo.

I keep that gal in business.
I've walked away from everywhere, left

lipstick smears through the Wild West
and Europe's iron heart.

Maybe staying still is a way of giving up
on yourself for someone else

and is in this way a kind of romance
that is beautiful because it is sad

like a tsarist Russian novel
in which there is dancing and suffering,

all that we are born to do.

Triskelion

What am I to do with what I have perfected—
    French braids, roshambo, the forging
of my father's signed name? A cowboy boot,

    he married in threes: a slide rule, a rosary,
the coupon box I crawled out of and in-
    to a life of Februarys, which is to say I'm still

alive, the gut and salt me, not even the papier-
    mâché one I dressed in yellow and steered
into the years. I am an easy impression:

    red hair, glasses, speak some Spanglish—
no one will know I'm not here. I've been gone
    before—lo, no search party torched for me

in the haystack night, thick with drums and tongues
    and flame. While I was waiting to be seen
a man thought I was a tree, invasive species, drilled

a copper nail into my skin, freckled
with attempted murders. Hollowed, I'm a host
    for grackle plagues coughing their razorblade

parade—they shit and strut, midnight dictators
    overthrowing my lungs but it's nice to be
a home, red barn on the picaresque horizon,

    blood sun scarring not the sky
but the eye that wants too long. I've been pinned
    to a door, a tree, pinned to the ocean,

the floor, lived under glass til the glass turned back
    to dust. Then I lived under that, too.
We have come to the part of the river's indecision—

    which way,
how strong,
    what for?

⁖ ACKNOWLEDGMENTS ⁖

Many thanks to the following journals in which these poems first appeared, sometimes in a different form:

> *Boulevard*: "The Jennifer Century"; *Crazyhorse*: "My Son, the Night Light, the Dark"; *Elbow Room NM*: "Pilgrimage"; *Florida Review*: "The Mammogram"; *Georgia Review*: "Of Yalta," "Pisces"; *Green Mountains Review*: "Afterbirth Abecedarian"; *Horsethief*: "The Confessions," "Lookback"; *Iowa Review Online*: "Once I Was a Thimble but Now I Am a Bell"; *Kenyon Review*: "I Am Twenty-One," "In the Black Forest," "Portrait of the Mother: 1985"; *Nimrod International Journal*: "Vow," "Natural History"; *The Pinch*: "I Would Have Listened to Rush," "Ode to My Dishwasher"; *Pleiades*: "Self-Portrait as Banshee"; *Prairie Schooner*: "Triskelion," "Twelve"; *Radar Poetry*: "Domestic Geography"; *Salt Hill Review*: "Rough Math"; *Squaw Valley Review*: "American Idyll"; *Superstition Review*: "Neighborhood Watch," "Regeneration," "The Trap"; *Whiskey Island*: "On a Line Overheard in a Crowd of Middle School Cheerleaders"; *Yes Poetry*: "A Murder of Librarians," "The New Year," "Seeing Ex-Boyfriends."

PBS NewsHour featured "The Jennifer Century" in January 2017.

Poetry Daily featured "Of Yalta" in April 2015.

"In a Dry County" first appeared as part of the Tupelo Press 30/30 in June 2016.

Thank you to Ed Ochester and all of the editors and staff at the Pitt Poetry Series and the University of Pittsburgh Press.

My undying gratitude goes to Rebecca Aronson, my poetry wife, for her faith, insight, and endless support. This book would not exist without her.

Thanks to my writing pen-pals Airea D. Matthews, Jennifer Hope Choi, Aaron Jacobs, and Graham Barnhart. For so long I went through the world without this—a communion of words and terrible jokes. I now expect nothing less. Thank you also to Amy Mullin, who was the original.

I am deeply indebted to those who welcomed me in to the writing community, particularly to Stephen Corey and Jenny Gropp Hess at the *Georgia Review*—thank you for opening the door. Gratitude also to the editors at *Radar*, *The Pinch*, and *Superstition Review* for their Pushcart Prize nominations and support.

I'm also grateful for the opportunities that allowed me to share my work and receive feedback. Thank you to those at the Bread Loaf Writers' Conference, the Community of Writers at Squaw Valley, the Rona Jaffe Foundation, Tin House Writer's

Workshop, and The Writer's Hotel. Thanks especially to those whose profound talent and generosity have shed new light on what it was my writing could do, including: Don Mee Choi, Michael Collier, Stephen Dunn, Robert Hass, Tony Hoagland, Valerie Martinez, Harryette Mullen, Antonia Nelson, Matthew Olzmann, Maggie Smith, Natasha Trethewey, Kevin Young, and Matthew Zapruder; also to the late Steve Orlen and C.D. Wright.

To the many whose love and friendship urged me to not quit, especially: Tomas Aguilar, Beth Borts, Christie Chisholm, Gina Corpening, Josh Fox, Lisa Hase Jackson & Gary Jackson, Marissa Juarez, Allison May, Virginia Miller, Trish O'Connor, Jennifer Schaller, the *Alibi* women and the Las Cruces crew.

Thanks to Yvette Montoya and Mike Wolff for their cameras and kindness.

Love to my family—all of you, in all your cracked splendor, but especially Robin Adair, Ron Hodges, Kourtney Hodges, Joshua Hodges, Melissa Neal, Sean Gabaldon, and Paula Hodges, as well as Anne and Cesar Garcia. I appreciate you whether you like it or not.

And to Sean and Theo, of course: for everything and for always.